Where Is Florida?

Where Is Florida?

by Jennifer Marino Walters

illustrated by Ted Hammond

Penguin Workshop

To Mom and Dad. Thank you for believing
in me from that very first short story!—JMW

PENGUIN WORKSHOP
An imprint of Penguin Random House LLC
1745 Broadway, New York, NY 10019
penguinrandomhouse.com

Copyright © 2025 by Penguin Random House LLC

Designed and Produced by Dinardo Design, LLC.

Library of Congress Cataloging-in-Publication Data is available.

First published in the United States of America by Penguin Workshop, 2025

Manufactured in the United States of America
CJKW

ISBN 9798217051373 (paperback)
10 9 8 7 6 5 4 3 2 1

ISBN 9798217051380 (library binding)
10 9 8 7 6 5 4 3 2 1

The authorized representative in the EU for product safety and compliance is
Penguin Random House Ireland, Morrison Chambers, 32 Nassau Street,
Dublin D02 YH68, Ireland, https://eu-contact.penguin.ie.

Contents

Where Is Florida?

On the morning of May 5, 1961, half a million people gathered on beaches near Florida's Cape Canaveral Air Force Station (now Cape Canaveral Space Force Station) to watch a once-in-a-lifetime event. About forty-five million Americans were glued to their television sets. Even President John F. Kennedy was watching TV from the White House!

People anxiously awaited the launch of the National Aeronautics and Space Administration (NASA) Redstone 3 rocket. The rocket would carry a Mercury capsule called *Freedom 7* into outer space. Inside would be an astronaut, Alan Shepard.

The flight was delayed for more than two hours because of technical difficulties. As the minutes

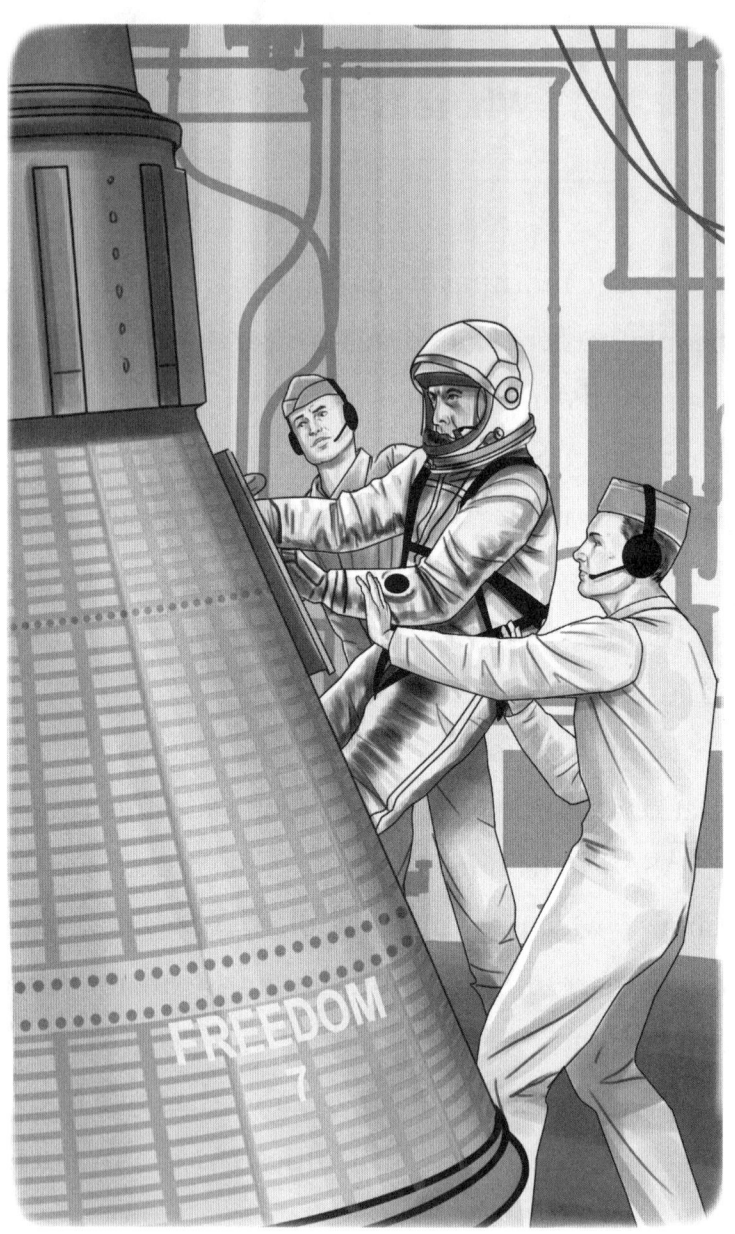

ticked by, people wondered: What's taking so long? Will the rocket take off?

At 9:34 a.m., it finally did, launching Shepard into space and into history books. Shepard was the first American ever to go to space. The fifteen-minute, twenty-eight-second flight was a huge achievement for the US space program.

Eight years later, the US space program put the first human on the moon—and he took off from Florida!

CHAPTER 1
Florida's Land, Coasts, and Environment

Florida is the southernmost state on the US mainland. About two-thirds of the state lies on a peninsula (a piece of land surrounded by water on three sides). It is bordered by the Atlantic Ocean to the east, the Gulf of Mexico to the west, and the Straits of Florida and Cuba to the south. Alabama is to its northwest, Georgia to its north.

The Florida Keys are a chain of over 1,700 small islands off the southern tip of the peninsula. The Keys stretch about 200 miles. About forty of these tropical islands are connected by bridges.

When it comes to land area, Florida is not particularly big. At 65,758 square miles, it's only the twenty-second-largest US state. Population-wise, however, Florida is the third-largest state in the country, after California and Texas, as of 2023.

Florida is the flattest state in the United States. Much of its land is made of sedimentary rock, which forms when sand, mud, and pebbles get pressed together and harden over millions of years. Most of Florida lies less than one hundred feet above sea level. The only hills in Florida are along its border with Georgia and Alabama in the northern part of the state.

Most of Florida is coastal plain (a flat, low-lying piece of land next to the ocean). Florida has over 8,400 miles of shoreline, second only to Alaska. In fact, no point in Florida is more than 60 miles from a coast! Different areas of Florida's seaside have unique features and cultures. These coastal regions even have fun nicknames.

In northeastern Florida is the First Coast—the first part of the coast you reach when entering Florida from Georgia. Duval County, including

Jacksonville, the largest city by area in the continental United States, covers 875 square miles and is part of the First Coast.

South of the First Coast is the Space Coast, the hub of the US space program. NASA and other space companies build, test, and launch rockets at the Kennedy Space Center on Merritt Island and at the Cape Canaveral Space Force Station. The Space Coast is also famous for another activity—surfing! Cocoa Beach is known as the surfing capital of the East Coast and boasts the world's largest surf shop, Ron Jon Surf Shop.

Further south is the Treasure Coast, named for the shipwrecks that took place in its waters. These include eleven Spanish ships that were wrecked during a hurricane in 1715 while carrying gold, silver, gemstones, and other treasures. The ships remained mostly undisturbed in the water for over two hundred years until silver and other items began to wash up on the beach. People

started to scuba dive to the shipwrecks to hunt for treasure. Since then, many thousands of artifacts and treasures have been discovered.

The Treasure Coast is home to Indian River Lagoon. The lagoon is actually an estuary, or an area where a river flows into the ocean. In fact, it's the most biologically diverse estuary in North America, which means it has the most individual species living in it. Indian River Lagoon has over four thousand species of animals and plants! Blowing Rocks Preserve on Jupiter Island is also part of the Treasure Coast. There, columns of salt water sometimes shoot as many as fifty feet into the sky through holes in the limestone rock.

The western coast of Florida (part of the US Gulf Coast) is known for its white sand beaches and aqua or emerald-green water. The northwestern part of the state is called the Florida Panhandle, because it's a narrow strip of land extending from the larger state of Florida, resembling the handle of a cooking pan. The Panhandle is home to the Marianna lowlands, full of limestone caves and sinkholes (areas where water has caused the limestone to cave in, forming a hole in the ground). The Panhandle also has the state's highest point, Britton Hill. At only 345 feet above sea level, it's the lowest "high point" of any state.

Everglades National Park lies at the southern tip of the Florida peninsula. This park includes 1.5 million acres of swampy marshland full of all sorts of wildlife, from manatees to Florida panthers to wading birds such as egrets. A lot of the watery land is covered with saw grass, a type of wild plant that grows up to fifteen feet tall. Everglades National Park is the only place in the world where both alligators and crocodiles live together in the wild. The Everglades used to be much bigger. In the past, people drained parts of

Great egret

the Everglades to grow crops. They built levees (long walls of soil that help prevent flooding) and canals to make room for farms and houses. In 1947, Everglades National Park was created to protect what was left of this unique habitat.

In addition to its coastline, Florida has over 7,700 lakes, about 1,700 streams, and over 1,000 freshwater springs. Lake Okeechobee (say: ow-kee-CHOW-bee) is located at the northern edge of the Everglades in south-central Florida and is the state's largest freshwater lake. Even though it's big, it's shallow—an average of only nine feet deep. That makes it a great home for wading birds, among other species. Dry Tortugas National Park in the Gulf of Mexico and Biscayne National Park in the northern Florida Keys are both over 90 percent covered by water.

Florida is home to the only living coral barrier reef in the continental United States. Corals may look like plants or rocks but are actually made up of small marine animals called polyps (say: PA-lips). They are connected to one another, stay in one place, and have hard skeletons. Like a beehive has thousands of bees, corals have many thousands of polyps—and reefs have thousands of corals. A coral reef is a living community! A barrier reef is a reef that forms in open water. The Florida Reef extends over 350 miles.

Most of Florida has a humid subtropical climate, which means hot summers and mild winters. Southern Florida has a tropical climate, which means it's humid and warm year-round, with lots of rain. It's rarely very cold for long anywhere in the state. In fact, Florida is one of the hottest and most humid US states. Florida also gets lots of sun: There are about 250 days of sunshine each year! That's why Florida is nicknamed the Sunshine State. The nickname doesn't tell the whole story: Florida also has more thunderstorms and hurricanes than any other state.

Florida Hurricanes

A hurricane is a strong storm that starts in the ocean with heavy rain and winds of at least seventy-four miles per hour. A hurricane begins when a tropical depression (a line of weak storms circling around an area of low air pressure) forms in the ocean. The low air pressure causes warm air that evaporates (turns into water vapor) from the ocean's surface to rise in a spiral. Because it draws

on warm air and water, a hurricane usually starts over tropical oceans. As the air rises, it cools down and condenses (becomes more compact) into large storm clouds. The low-pressure area continues to suck up warm, moist air, making the spiral faster and stronger.

Hurricanes can produce winds of over 150 miles per hour. Winds that strong can destroy homes and damage roads and bridges. They also bring seawater in to flood neighborhoods and cities.

Florida generally experiences hurricanes between June and November. The deadliest Florida hurricane was the Okeechobee Hurricane of 1928. It made landfall near West Palm Beach and killed over 2,500 people. In 2004, four hurricanes pummeled Florida in only six weeks. In 2024, Hurricane Milton made landfall on Florida's west coast with winds of up to 180 miles per hour, making it one of the strongest Atlantic hurricanes ever recorded.

More than three hundred types of native trees grow in Florida. This includes mangroves (tropical trees with roots growing from their branches), apple and cherry trees, and over a dozen types of palm trees, some of which can grow to be over sixty feet tall. There are also about four thousand species of beautiful native plants, including some less beautiful species that are still important. The Florida ziziphus may look tough with two-inch-long thorns, but this shrub from central Florida is critically endangered.

The state animal, the Florida panther, is also endangered. Florida's waters are home to many manatees, bottlenose dolphins, northern right whales, and other marine mammals (mammals that live in the ocean). The Florida scrub jay is a bird found only in the Sunshine State. Even wild hogs roam throughout Florida!

CHAPTER 2
State Origins

Indigenous nations first entered the area now known as Florida as many as twelve thousand years ago. Hunters and gatherers who came from the north, they lived mainly on animals they caught and ate. They also collected plants, nuts, and shellfish. They made weapons and tools out of stone. After 500 BCE, Indigenous peoples continued to come to Florida from the north in smaller numbers. They farmed crops like corn, squash, and beans. By the time Europeans arrived in the Florida region in the 1500s, hundreds of thousands of Indigenous people lived there, including Apalachee, Timucua, Ais, Tocobaga, and Calusa peoples.

Spanish explorer Juan Ponce de León was the

first European to reach Florida. Looking for gold and other resources, he landed on the peninsula in spring of 1513. He named it *La Florida* (Spanish for "land of flowers") in celebration of a Spanish Easter tradition.

For decades, Spanish explorers tried and failed to set up colonies in Florida. In 1564, a group of French Protestants (a branch of Christianity) established Fort Caroline near present-day Jacksonville. Spain traded weapons, tools, and other goods to Cuba, in exchange for sugar and tobacco. Spain didn't want France attacking their ships from Fort Caroline. To drive out the French, a Spanish settlement called St. Augustine was established in 1565. Some of the settlers brought enslaved African people with them, marking the beginnings of slavery in Florida. Soon after arriving, the group killed most of the French colonists and many Indigenous people. Today, St. Augustine is the country's oldest city that has been continually lived in since its founding.

Spain controlled Florida for the next two hundred years. They set up missions (religious settlements) to try to convert the Timucua and Apalachee peoples and other Indigenous groups to Christianity. Some Indigenous people living in and around these missions were enslaved or forced to do work for the Spanish, mainly on farms. In the 1650s, many Timucua people rebelled against the Spanish military and tried to take back their land. The rebellion was unsuccessful. Many Timucua people also died from diseases like smallpox, brought over by the Europeans.

The British also wanted to claim Florida as their own. They often attacked it. In 1762, they took control of Havana, Cuba. Cuba was still an important trade partner to Spain. Spain traded ownership of Florida to England for Havana.

The British brought thousands of enslaved African people to Florida. Most were forced to work on farms, growing and picking cotton, sugar, corn, and other crops. They also worked in citrus groves (groups of trees that produce fruit) that grew fruits like oranges, lemons, limes, and grapefruits.

By the mid-1700s, almost all the Indigenous peoples in Florida, including the Timucua and the Calusa, died from diseases, or were killed or enslaved by the British. Many members of an Indigenous nation called the Muscogee (called the Creeks by British settlers) began moving from Georgia and Alabama to Florida because Europeans were taking over their lands. They were accompanied by enslaved Africans seeking freedom and a few white settlers. This group of people formed a community and eventually came to be known as the Seminole people.

At the end of the American Revolutionary War in 1783, a peace treaty returned Florida to Spain. The United States began claiming parts of Florida in the early 1800s. At the same time, the Seminole Nation fought to keep control of their land. The First Seminole War took place from 1817 to 1818. US troops led by General Andrew Jackson captured Pensacola in northwest Florida.

The Seminole people who lived there were forced to move farther south.

Spain agreed to transfer Florida to the United States in 1819. They officially took control of the region, and Tallahassee was named its capital. In

1832, a small number of Seminole people signed the Treaty of Payne's Landing. That treaty required Seminole people to give up their land in Florida and move to Oklahoma. Seminole leader Osceola and his followers refused to give up their land. This

led to the Second Seminole War (1835–1842). Osceola and his people were defeated. By the end of the war most were relocated to Oklahoma.

Florida became the twenty-seventh US state on March 3, 1845. The few hundred Seminole people still in Florida struggled to hold on to their remaining land, and the Third Seminole War took place from 1855 to 1858. When the war ended, only about two hundred Seminole people remained in the state.

The Union and the Confederacy fought each other in the American Civil War from 1861 to 1865, mainly over the issue of slavery. The Union wanted to end slavery, and the Confederacy wanted slavery to continue. Florida joined ten other Southern states (South Carolina, Mississippi, Alabama, Georgia, Louisiana, Texas, Virginia, Arkansas, North Carolina, and Tennessee) to form the Confederacy. More than twenty states in the North, upper South, West, and Midwest formed the Union, led by President Abraham Lincoln.

The Union won the war. In 1865, the Thirteenth Amendment to the US Constitution officially outlawed slavery. The United States worked to bring the former Confederate states back into the Union. Florida began to rebuild coastal cities and towns that had been damaged during the war.

Wealthy people realized that Florida could become a popular tourist destination—especially in winter—because of its warm weather and sunny beaches. They began to buy up land in the state. One of them was Henry M. Flagler.

Although he was born in New York, Flagler was called the "father" of modern-day Florida. In 1885, he began work to improve a railroad along Florida's northeast Atlantic coast. Flagler also built hotels along the route. A railroad route on Florida's western side had begun the year before.

By 1912, the Florida East Coast Railway extended all the way down to Key West. Florida was now connected to cities in South Carolina, Georgia, and Alabama, as well as even further north. The Sunshine State was on its way to becoming a vacation destination.

CHAPTER 3
Growth and Development

The development of railroads, hotels, and houses led to huge growth. In the late 1800s and early 1900s, many people from northern states moved to Florida, away from the cold and snow. Immigrants from northern Spain and Italy came during and after the period of World War I (1914–1918). During World War II (1939–1945), Florida's warm weather helped it become a major training center for pilots, soldiers, and sailors.

Post-war changes brought money and development to Florida. Cities grew and schools improved. But in the 1950s, Black people living in Florida still did not have equal rights or access to some of these resources. Segregation (the separation of Black people and white people in public places) was the law. Black and white children attended separate schools. Black people had to sit in the back of city buses. All over the state, Black people fought for equal rights and better treatment.

One such fight was the Tallahassee Bus Boycott of 1956. A boycott is when a group of people choose not to spend money at a certain business to show they will not support its rules. On May 26, two African American students from Florida Agricultural and Mechanical University (FAMU) boarded a bus and sat in the only open seats, which were in the "whites only" section. They were ordered to move to the back of the bus. When they refused, they were arrested.

After that, many African Americans in Tallahassee refused to ride city buses. They didn't want to give their money to a bus service that discriminated against them. The boycott

continued until December 22, 1956, when the Supreme Court ruled that segregation on city buses was unconstitutional. Black civil rights activists tested the decision by sitting in the front

of the Tallahassee city buses, and by 1957, the buses were integrated.

Cuban people also came to Florida in large numbers. After the Cuban Revolution in 1959,

Fidel Castro became the leader of Cuba. He turned Cuba into a Communist nation. Communism is a type of government in which individual people do not own land, factories, or machinery. Instead, the government or community owns these things. Everyone is supposed to share equally. Under Castro, though, those who opposed Communism or his way of leading were punished or killed. The media was censored. Large numbers of Cubans began to escape, and many went to Florida.

A steady stream of Cuban immigrants settled in the United States, many of them in Miami. People from other Latin American countries, like Colombia and Nicaragua, also came to Florida to work in its citrus groves and on farms.

In the 1950s and '60s, there was another Communist country that changed history in Florida: the Soviet Union. The United States and the Soviet Union believed rockets and space exploration would be an important part of the future. Both countries raced to be the first to the moon. The first American space rocket with people on board launched from Cape Canaveral in 1961. Astronaut Alan Shepard became the first American to go to space. The Kennedy Space Center (originally called the Launch Operations Center) opened a year later on Merritt Island.

On July 16, 1969, astronauts Neil Armstrong, Buzz Aldrin, and Michael Collins blasted off from the Kennedy Space Center aboard the Apollo 11 capsule on the Saturn V rocket. Four days later, Armstrong became the first person to step foot on the moon.

Anything seemed possible in Florida. Walt Disney even chose it as the location for his new theme park. He began purchasing land near Orlando for the park in 1965. Unfortunately, Walt Disney died before he got to see his dream become a reality.

The Most Magical Place on Earth

When Walt Disney World opened on October 1, 1971, there was only one theme park (Magic Kingdom). Today, Walt Disney World Resort includes four theme parks, two water parks, and more than twenty-five hotels! It also has golf courses, campgrounds, a sports complex, and Disney Springs (a fun area full of stores, restaurants, and more).

At Epcot theme park, visitors can experience the food and culture of various countries like Japan, Mexico, and Italy without leaving the United States! At Hollywood Studios—originally called Disney-MGM Studios—guests can fly the *Millennium Falcon* (just watch out for stormtroopers!). Animal Kingdom offers open-air safari rides past roaming zebras, elephants, giraffes, and other animals. And water parks Typhoon Lagoon and Blizzard Beach have all sorts of waterslides and splash areas.

Today, Magic Kingdom gets more visitors each year than any other theme park in the world. Over seventeen million people visited the Magic Kingdom in 2023!

Florida's theme parks soon expanded beyond Disney. SeaWorld Orlando is a theme park, aquarium, and zoo all in one and now has eleven hotels and a water park. Universal Orlando Resort is home to Marvel Super Hero Island, DreamWorks Land, Seuss Landing, and more. Universal Orlando Resort also has a water park, ten hotels, and an entertainment district called CityWalk, full of shops, restaurants, and more.

Legoland Florida Resort is in Winter Haven, about a forty-five-minute drive from the Orlando theme parks. It includes Legoland Theme Park, Legoland Water Park, three themed hotels, and Peppa Pig Theme Park.

All of these theme parks, plus fantastic beaches and abundant wildlife, make Florida a family vacation destination for people around the world. Over 140 million people visited the state in 2023. Of those, more than 11 million came from outside the United States. In fact, Florida is frequently one of the most-visited states by international travelers, making it a symbol of American life around the world.

CHAPTER 4
Today's State

Today, Florida has the fourth-largest economy of all the US states, after California, Texas, and New York. Tourism is the biggest part of Florida's economy, and many people who live there work in theme parks, hotels, and restaurants. Florida's beach towns are also popular with tourists. The Port of Miami is the largest cruise port in the world!

Florida is the country's largest producer of orange juice, with citrus groves located throughout the state, including central Florida and the east and west coasts. It also produces more mangoes, sugarcane, and watermelons than any other state. Other big Florida crops include grapefruit, corn, strawberries, and peppers.

Florida produces more than just fruits and vegetables. The state manufactures computers and other electronics. Transportation equipment, chemicals, and wood products are also made in the Sunshine State.

Going to the beach is a way of life in many coastal parts of Florida, and the Orlando area is known for its theme parks. Yet there is so much more to Florida. The state is famous for its many golf courses and tennis courts. Florida has over 1,200 golf courses—more than any other state. The Ladies Professional Golf Association (LPGA) is headquartered in Daytona Beach. Many major golf tournaments take place in Florida.

Other sports are big in Florida, too! In addition to Florida's own two Major League Baseball (MLB) teams (the Miami Marlins and the Tampa Bay Rays), thirteen other MLB teams have spring training camps in Florida. When it's still too cold for baseball in places like Boston and Detroit, the teams move south to practice in Florida! The state also has two National Hockey League teams (the Tampa Bay Lightning and the Florida Panthers) and two National Basketball Association teams (the Miami Heat and the Orlando Magic). Florida's Major League Soccer team, Inter Miami, began in 2020.

NASCAR is headquartered in Daytona Beach, and the Daytona 500 takes place there each

February. This major car race is five hundred miles long! Each year, over one hundred thousand people head to the Daytona International Speedway to watch and cheer on their favorite drivers.

While Florida has three National Football League teams—the Tampa Bay Buccaneers, the Miami Dolphins, and the Jacksonville Jaguars—college football is also popular in the state. The annual Orange Bowl, played in January, is always held in the Miami area.

Floridians don't only have sports to watch—they can visit museums, too. Circus Museum in Sarasota features circus history, both past and present. Gainesville's Florida Museum of Natural History has loads of fossils and a butterfly rainforest. The Vizcaya Museum and Gardens in Miami is a 1916 historic home with thirty-two furnished rooms and ten acres of gorgeous gardens. Miami's Wynwood Art District features street art on over eighty thousand square feet of walls.

There are also many colleges and universities in Florida. The State University System of Florida has twelve public universities. Florida is also home to the University of Miami in Coral Gables and the Florida Institute of Technology in Melbourne. The state's first private university was Stetson University in DeLand, founded in 1883.

It's no surprise that so many artists, athletes, and famous thinkers are from Florida. Singer and actress Ariana Grande was born in Boca Raton. Actor Josh Gad, who voiced the lovable snowman Olaf in *Frozen*, is from Hollywood, Florida. Author Carl Hiaasen grew up in Plantation, Florida, and still lives in the state. And former NFL running back Emmitt Smith is from Pensacola.

Because of its fantastic weather, many people move to Florida when they retire. No more shoveling snow! Florida has one of the highest percentages of people over age sixty-five of any state—around 20 percent—and only about 35 percent of Florida residents were born there.

There are also Indigenous groups that call Florida home. The Seminole Nation is in Florida. There are more than two thousand Seminole people living in the state today. Many Seminole people live on reservations, or areas of land that are governed by the Seminole Nation. There are six Seminole reservations in the state.

Florida is home to more people of Cuban background than any other state. Of the roughly two million people of Cuban ancestry in the United States, more than 60 percent live in Florida. Most of Florida's Cuban population lives in and around Miami. Cuban food, music, and traditions are strong in the area. Miami's Little Havana neighborhood has restaurants serving

Cuban food and shops selling Cuban clothing and décor. The largest Latin music festival in the United States, Calle Ocho, takes place there every March.

Miami and Tampa are rivals for which city makes the best Cuban sandwich, which usually includes ham, roast pork, Swiss cheese, pickles, and mustard. Florida isn't known only for Cuban food. It's also famous for seafood, including conch fritters and stone crab. Visitors often sample Key lime pie, which reportedly was invented in Florida.

Whether exploring the Everglades and searching for alligators, or watching a rocket take off from Cape Canaveral, the sky is the limit when it comes to Florida!

Florida at a Glance

Statehood: 1845

Nickname: The Sunshine State

Abbreviation: FL

State Motto:
In God We Trust

State Tree: Sabal palm

State Animal: Panther

Capital: Tallahassee

Size: 65,758 square miles

Population: More than 23 million

Famous People from Florida:

Pitbull (rapper and singer),

Bob Ross (artist), Deion Sanders

(NFL player), Bella Thorne

(actress), Janet Reno (first female

US attorney general)

★ Tallahassee

State flag

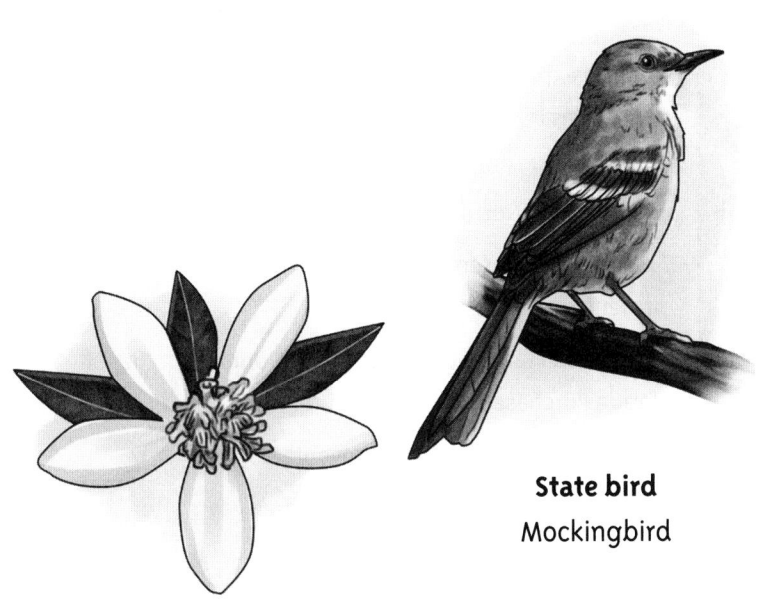

State bird
Mockingbird

State flower
Orange blossom

FUN FACT:

Florida spans two time zones! Ten counties in the northern and western part of Florida, known as the Panhandle, observe Central Time. The rest of the state observes Eastern Time.

Timeline of Florida

1513 — Spanish explorer Juan Ponce de León lands in Florida and claims it for Spain

1565 — St. Augustine, the oldest permanent European settlement in North America, is founded

1763 — Spain trades present-day Florida to Britain for present-day Havana, Cuba

1819 — The United States regains control of Florida with the Florida Purchase Treaty

1845 — Florida becomes the twenty-seventh US state

1868 — Florida is readmitted to the Union three years after the American Civil War ends

1912 — Henry Flagler's oversea railroad to Key West is completed

1947 — Everglades National Park is established

1961 — Alan Shepard blasts off from the Cape Canaveral Space Center and becomes the first American in space

1971 — Walt Disney World opens in Orlando

2004 — Four hurricanes hit Florida in a six-week period

2024 — Hurricane Milton slams Florida with winds up to 180 miles per hour, making it one of the strongest Atlantic hurricanes ever recorded

Timeline of the World

1508– 1512 — Michelangelo paints the ceiling of the Sistine Chapel in Vatican City, Italy

1558 — Elizabeth I becomes queen of England

1631 — Construction begins on India's Taj Mahal

1783 — The first piloted hot-air balloon flight occurs over Paris

1821 — Mexico declares independence from Spain

1867 — The United States buys the territory of Alaska from Russia

1912 — The RMS *Titanic* sinks on its maiden voyage from England; about 1,500 people drown

1941 — Japan attacks a US fleet at Pearl Harbor in Hawaii, bringing the United States into World War II

1957 — Russia launches the first Earth-orbiting satellite, Sputnik 1

1963 — Martin Luther King Jr. delivers his famous "I Have a Dream" speech in Washington, DC

2001 — On September 11, terrorists hijack and crash two airplanes into New York City's Twin Towers

2024 — The Congo River rises to its highest level in sixty years, causing flooding throughout the Democratic Republic of Congo and killing more than three hundred people

Bibliography

*Books for young readers

*Alexander, Heather. *Only in Florida: Weird and Wonderful Facts About The Sunshine State.* London, UK: Wide-Eyed Editions, 2024.

*Holub, Joan. *Where Is Walt Disney World?* New York: Penguin Workshop, 2018.

*Orr, Tamra B. *Florida.* A True Book: My United States. New York: Scholastic Inc., 2018.

Websites

Florida Department of State Facts for Kids:
dos.fl.gov/florida-facts/kids

Official website of Cape Canaveral Space Force Station:
www.patrick.spaceforce.mil

Official website of Everglades National Park:
www.nps.gov/ever/index.htm

Official website of the Kennedy Space Center:
www.kennedyspacecenter.com

Visit Florida: www.visitflorida.com